Drug Abuse and Society™

GHB AND ANALOGS
High-Risk Club Drugs

The Rosen Publishing Group, Inc., New York

Marie E. Wolf

This book is dedicated to parents everywhere who have lost a child to drugs. May their generosity in telling their tragic stories save others.

Published in 2007 by The Rosen Publishing Group, Inc.
29 East 21st Street, New York, NY 10010

First Edition

Library of Congress Cataloging-in-Publication Data

Wolf, Marie (Marie E.)
GHB and analogs: high-risk club drugs / Marie Wolf.—1st ed.
   p. cm.—(Drug abuse and society)
Includes bibliographical references and index.
ISBN-13: 978-1-4042-0910-7
ISBN-10: 1-4042-0910-7 (library binding)
1. Gamma hydroxybutyrate—Juvenile literature.
I. Title. II. Series.
RM666.G127W65 2007
615'.782—dc22

2006012872

Manufactured in the United States of America

Contents

INTRODUCTION

Gamma hydroxybutyrate (GHB)—known on the street as "Georgia Home Boy" and "Liquid X"—is a popular party drug. It is classified by law in the United States as a Schedule I Controlled Substance. This means it falls into the category of the most dangerous drugs, having no legitimate medical use and a high potential for abuse.

A central nervous system depressant, GHB has become the drug of choice for teens who want to shake off their inhibitions and party non-stop at clubs and raves. Bodybuilders and athletes looking to trim fat and build muscle also abuse this illegal drug. In addition, GHB has become known as a date-rape drug. People have easily slipped the substance into the drink of an unsuspecting companion or random

Gamma hydroxybutyrate (GHB) is a clear, liquid substance that looks just like water. It is sold illegally, usually in vials, small plastic bottles, or by the capful. Users often sip it from plastic soft-drink bottles. Since it is odorless, colorless, and tasteless, users can avoid detection by pretending it is water or mixing it with other beverages. It is less often sold and consumed as a light-colored powder.

stranger, rendering the victim unconscious and unable to fend off a sexual attack or encounter.

Today, this clear, liquid substance is showing up at community functions that have been promoted as alcohol-free. Unsuspecting parents send their teens to such events, where they assume the only beverages their kids will be consuming are soft drinks.

Unlike alcohol, however, GHB is odorless and therefore undetectable on someone's breath.

GHB has found its way onto university campuses across the United States. According to Brown University's Health Education Web site, club drugs, including GHB, have become some of the fastest-growing drugs used by college students.

GHB is taken orally (through the mouth) and is produced in liquid or powder form. It has a slightly salty taste, which is masked when mixed with a soft drink or alcohol. According to the U.S. Drug Enforcement Administration (DEA), GHB is sold by the capful. Prices range from $5 to $25 per cap. The drug is manufactured illegally in private homes right in the kitchen or in makeshift basement laboratories—often using unsafe recipes found on the Internet.

GHB is temptingly affordable for teens looking for a cheap high who may not care how pure the ingredients are. However, that is where the danger lies. In many cases, GHB is produced using a similar, yet less expensive ingredient such as GBL (gamma butyrolactone), an industrial solvent that is an analog or "chemical cousin" to GHB. Once ingested, GBL is converted to GHB. It creates the same effects, but unfortunately, users have no clue that they have just swallowed industrial cleaner.

Most recreational GHB users are unaware of the clearly documented physical and psychological dangers of the drug. Users claim that the benefits of taking the drug in low doses range from feelings of euphoria (extreme happiness), relaxation, and increased sexual desire, to weight loss and a good night's sleep. The facts, however—gathered by health professionals and drug enforcement officials—point to many adverse, or harmful, reactions.

When consumed in high doses, GHB can cause vomiting, violent outbursts, hallucinations, unconsciousness, seizures, or coma. Taken with alcohol, it can be deadly. Although GHB was once sold legally in health food stores in the United States as a body-building dietary supplement, it was banned in the early 1990s by the U.S. Food and Drug Administration (FDA). The FDA offered overwhelming evidence that GHB misuse was responsible for growing medical problems and, in some cases, death.

If you are curious about GHB and are tempted to try it, you should research the drug and its effects for yourself. It is illegal to buy it, sell it, consume it, or slip it into someone else's drink and trick them into consuming it. Scientists are still studying the long-term effects of GHB abuse, but they already believe it is capable of altering memory and learning functions. Lastly, you should always remain aware that GHB can make you pass out, leaving you vulnerable to sexual assault and rape. You may become so physically incapacitated that you would be unable to resist, fight back, or even be aware of what is happening to you.

CHAPTER 1
The History of GHB

In 1960, gamma hydroxybutyrate (GHB) was introduced in France as an anesthetic agent—something that dulls pain and sensation. It was developed by Dr. Henri Laborit, who was searching for an alternative drug to aid in surgery. GHB was known to induce sleep, but it did little to reduce pain. Therefore, its use in surgery ceased.

During the 1980s, in health food stores across the United States, GHB was sold over the counter to consumers hoping to benefit from the many alleged benefits of the substance. Touted as an alternative to steroids, it caught the attention of bodybuilders and athletes who wanted a "ripped" look—more muscle mass, less fat. Those with sleep disorders purchased GHB as a sleep aid. Dieters hoping to drop a few pounds were also interested in the drug, as were older adults

In 1960, Dr. Henri Laborit, a French neurologist, developed gamma hyroxybutyrate (GHB). He hoped it would be an effective anesthetic—something that would dull patients' pain during surgery. GHB induced sleep but failed as a pain reliever, so ultimately it was not used in surgery.

seeking an anti-aging formula. It was also advertised as an anti-depressant and as an aphrodisiac (a substance that increases sex drive).

THE BAN

As the use of GHB increased, so did the incidence of dangerous reactions. Growing reports of overdoses and deaths associated with products containing GHB were submitted to the FDA. After investigating the reports, the agency banned the sale of GHB and ordered it off the shelves by the end of 1991. The Office of National Drug Control Policy (ONDCP) identified the following side effects associated with taking GHB:

• Nausea
• Vomiting

- Vertigo (dizziness)
- Hallucinations
- Seizures
- Amnesia
- Loss of consciousness
- Coma
- Death

Despite the ban and the disclosure of the potential health risks associated with using the substance, users continued to find ways to obtain GHB. To get around the ban, some manufacturers began to substitute ingredients, using GHB analogs that are used in industrial cleaners—GBL (gamma butyrolactone) and BD (1,4 butanediol).

Adverse reactions and overdoses continued. In 1999, newspapers reported the deaths of two teenaged girls: Hillory J. Farias, a seventeen-year-old high school student from La Porte, Texas, and Samantha Reid, a fifteen-year-old from Rockwood, Michigan. Both died in separate incidents after unknowingly consuming soft drinks laced with GHB. On February 18, 2000, the "Hillory J. Farias and Samantha Reid Date-Rape Prohibition Act of 1999" was signed into law. What did this mean for GHB? It gave the drug a Schedule I classification. This is reserved for the most dangerous substances that have the highest potential for abuse and no recognized medical value. The analog GBL was also named under this law as a controlled chemical.

Joshua Cole *(left)* stands trial, accused of slipping GHB into a soft drink Samantha Reid consumed at a party. Reid, a fifteen-year-old from Rockwood, Michigan, fell into a coma and died. Her father, Charles Reid *(right)*, listens during the trial's opening arguments.

GHB can still be used legally in other approved drugs, however. In 2002, the FDA approved the use of the drug Xyrem to treat patients afflicted with narcolepsy (a condition that causes sudden, spontaneous sleep), who also experience related attacks of cataplexy (weakening of muscles). Xyrem contains the active ingredient sodium oxybate, or GHB. Under the law, illegal use of Xyrem is subject to Schedule I penalties (the penalties associated with misuse of a Schedule I drug).

GHB GOES UNDERGROUND

Despite the media exposure and the government ban prompted by the deaths of Farias and Reid, the lure of GHB continued to grow and take root illegally. This not only occurred with bodybuilders and weight-watchers, but also with pleasure-seeking teens. Kids looking for a way to "chill" with their friends at parties, clubs, and raves

Once banned by law, GHB went underground, springing up at clubs and all-night dance parties called "raves." These parties, like the one shown above, are usually held in warehouses or lofts, where drugs flow and techno music blares. Some try to heighten the rave experience by ingesting GHB or other club drugs, believing it will make them more sociable and uninhibited.

heard about GHB's supposedly intoxicating, euphoric effects. Others began using it as a sedative, to bring them down and lessen the impact of stimulants such as methamphetamine and cocaine.

Once banned, GHB went underground. Dealers began selling it on the street and over the Internet. Because it is a clear, odorless liquid, GHB has been flagrantly sold in squirt bottles, small vials, and by the capful. Users can buy lollipops dipped in GHB. In some U.S. cities, GHB has been put into water guns and sold by the squirt. It is generally sold between $5 and $25 a dose and is also marketed in capsule, tablet, and powder form (which is snorted).

COMMON MYTHS AND FACTS ABOUT GHB

You may have heard things about GHB from friends that make it seem fun, appealing, and harmless. Before accepting these claims uncritically, give thought to the following:

Myth: GHB is safe if taken in small doses.
Fact: There is no safe dose of GHB. It has a different effect on each user, based on the purity and strength of the dosage and the individual's system. The effects vary each time it is used. Only a small increase in dosage can raise the drug's sedative effects to lethal levels. Also, since the drug is manufactured illegally by home chemists, the

strength can vary considerably. Users can never be sure of the strength of the dosage they are getting.

Myth: GHB is safe even if produced with its analogs GBL (gamma butyrolactone) or BD (1,4 butanediol).

Fact: GHB is not safe under any circumstances, and its analogs GBL and BD are not safe substitutes. GBL is a solvent used in paint stripper. The National Drug Intelligence Center reports that both GBL and BD, used to produce GHB, are the same ingredients used in fish tank cleaner, nail polish remover, and ink cartridge cleaner.

Myth: GHB is not addictive.

Fact: Severe addiction can occur when GHB is used daily in varying amounts within a period ranging from two months to three years. In one study, researchers found that withdrawal symptoms began between one and six hours after the last dose.

DOSAGE AND DANGERS

As noted earlier, there is no single safe dosage of GHB or its analogs. The following is presented to explain the typical effects users experience at various dosage levels.

- Less than one gram (0.35 ounce) of GHB reportedly brings on a feeling of relaxation and reduces inhibitions.

Also Known As . . .

You may be unfamiliar with GHB's chemical name, gamma hydroxybutyrate. However, you may have heard it referred to by one of these slick street names:

- Cherry Meth
- Fantasy
- G
- Georgia Home Boy
- Great Hormones at Bedtime
- Grievous Bodily Harm
- Liquid E
- Liquid Ecstasy
- Salty water
- Scoop
- Sleep-500
- Soap
- Vita-G
- Street names of the GHB analogs GBL and BD include Blue Nitro, Renewtrient, Revivarant, Firewater, Enliven, Weight Belt Cleaner, and Serenity.

Its effects, which can be felt within five to fifteen minutes, peak in approximately thirty minutes, according to a 2004 report in the *Journal of Psychoactive Drugs*.

- One to two grams (0.035–0.07 oz) intensifies a relaxed state and slows both respiration and heart rate. At this dosage, GHB can also affect motor coordination and balance and slow blood circulation.
- Two to four grams (0.07–0.141 oz) cause major interference with speech and motor control. A coma-like sleep may follow.
- GHB mixed with alcohol can be fatal. Unconsciousness, coma, and death are real possibilities.

CHAPTER 2
Users and Pushers: The Reality of GHB Abuse

The reasons behind someone's decision to use GHB, or any other illegal drug, seem to be universal, regardless of age, cultural background, financial standing, or gender. Drug users say they experiment to feel good, to have fun, and to be more sociable. Some may be depressed and want a "happy fix." Teens often do drugs to fit in with their peers, to try to look cool, and to mask their insecurities. Other people are simply bored with their lives and want to shake things up a bit.

In the case of GHB abuse, most reports describe users and pushers as ranging in age from thirteen to thirty years old. The drug is primarily abused by white, middle-class males, but is also abused by people from many other walks of life. These include teens who want to get high and

Because GHB is a clear, odorless liquid, it can easily be slipped into your drink by someone intending to sexually assault you. Be safe—order your own drink and never leave it unattended. Don't take a drink from a punch-bowl or accept a drink that's already been opened for you. If in doubt, consider carrying a drug testing kit with you, like the Drink Detective pictured above.

party; athletes looking to bulk up or enhance performance; and sexual predators looking for an easy way to incapacitate others and then commit rape.

The Monitoring the Future Study is conducted annually by the University of Michigan and funded by the National Institute on Drug Abuse (NIDA). Its main goal is to study changes in the beliefs, attitudes, and behaviors of American teenagers over time, in regards to a wide range of issues, including drug use. The study, which, among other things, tracks drug abuse among U.S. high school students, found GHB use among 0.5 percent of eighth-graders, 0.8 percent of tenth-graders, and 1.1 percent of twelfth-graders in 2005. "Use" was defined as at least one dose taken during the year preceding participation in the survey.

THE DARK SIDE

When people experiment with GHB, the results—far from harmless fun—are often dangerous, permanently disabling, and even fatal. Here are some stories of GHB abuse reported by the media in recent years:

- In 1999, five Michigan teens attending a house party wound up hospitalized after sharing a drink spiked with GHB. Three teenage girls at another house party in Metairie, Louisiana, downed eight shot glasses of the GHB analog Invigorate and were hospitalized in serious condition.
- In 2003, Mike Scarcella, a professional bodybuilder and former Mr. America, died at age thirty-nine. The cause was an enlarged heart brought on by high blood pressure and withdrawal symptoms from his addiction to GHB, which friends said he struggled with for years. He died in a psychiatric hospital in McKinney, Texas.

- In 2006, a twenty-two-year-old male from Spenard, Alaska, was sentenced to thirteen years in federal prison after pleading guilty to charges of bringing a form of GHB to a party in 2003. At the party, the drug was mixed in a drink and passed around. A sixteen-year-old girl died and two others were injured.
- An anonymous GHB user posted the following story on Checkyourself.com, a teen site devoted to issues surrounding drug and alcohol abuse: "I woke up the next morning at a stranger's house without my clothes on. I was nauseous and my body felt totally numb . . . I had no memory of what happened."

THE USER

Drug consultant Trinka Porrata has monitored GHB abuse for more than a decade. She is a former Los Angeles Police Department narcotics detective and president of Project GHB, an Internet site that provides information and support for teens, parents, educators, and others who want to learn more about the drug. Porrata learned that GHB addicts dose in one of two ways:

1. Precise dosing in regular intervals separated by one to three hours, with slightly higher doses at night for sleep.

2. Around the clock sipping from a bottle of diluted (or watered down) product.

Neither method of dosing is safe. Effects from precise dosing can fluctuate based on variations in dosage and the amount or lack of food ingested. Sipping often results in overdose.

In an advisory released in November 2002 by the Substance Abuse and Mental Health Services Administration (SAMHSA), forty-two regular GHB users described the drug's effects. Users described euphoria, increased sex drive, and a calm, peaceful feeling. However, they also experienced sweating, headaches, fatigue, amnesia (loss of memory), confusion, clumsiness, nausea and vomiting, hallucinations, hearing things, and loss of consciousness.

Despite the overwhelming number of unpleasant and harmful reactions, the study reported that GHB users still touted the drug's perceived positive qualities. Yet family members described personality changes in loved ones who abused GHB. They noticed increased irritability, aggression, and poor memory.

THE PUSHER

Pushers are people who sell illegal drugs and try to get others hooked on their products. What's the pushers' bottom line? On the street, they want to make money. They often cut corners to make a buck. Even those without a background in chemistry can create batches of GHB in their homes, using recipe kits purchased on the Internet. If the drug is poorly formulated, however, users can suffer from severe burns to the mouth, throat, and esophagus.

Those who supply athletes with GHB may not consider themselves drug pushers. They think they are offering a magic potion that will enhance performance, burn fat, and build powerful muscles. But no one is immune from prosecution, even in the world of professional sports. In November 2005, Pete Rose Jr., son of the legendary baseball player, plead guilty to charges of distributing the GHB analog GBL to his minor league teammates. The punishment could cost him up to $1 million in fines and a jail term of up to two years.

RECOGNIZING A PROBLEM

Is GHB becoming a problem for you or someone you know? The following signs may indicate GHB abuse, according to the health education page of Brown University's Web site:

- You use the drug a lot.
- You have to keep increasing the dosage to get the usual effect.
- You are preoccupied with thoughts of using it.
- You spend more money than you have in order to get the drug.
- You start to cut classes and don't complete assignments.

- You find new friends who also use GHB and drop friends who don't.
- You find it difficult to relax or be happy without using the drug.
- You can't sleep without using it.

GHB—MORE WIDESPREAD THAN YOU THINK

"The typical user is the guy in the gym," says drug consultant Trinka Porrata in an interview with the author. "Kids who work out in the gym still think it builds muscle. Other body-builders are telling them, 'It puts you to sleep and you blossom,'" says Porrata. This is a myth carried over from

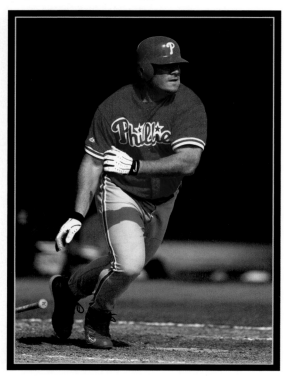

Pete Rose Jr. *(left)*, son of former Major League Baseball star Pete Rose, was arrested in 2005 and 2006 for distributing gamma butyrolactone (GBL) to fellow teammates on his minor league baseball team. GBL is a chemical compound similar to GHB that is used as a "steroid alternative." Rose was convicted and sentenced to one month in federal prison.

the days when GHB was sold over the counter in health food stores and advertised as a steroid alternative and growth hormone. Such users see GHB as an enhancer. "Some take it to go to sleep. Others take it with massive amounts of caffeine or ephedrine so that they won't go to sleep. Instead, they work out extra hard and they don't feel it [the exhaustion]."

Bodybuilders are not the only abusers of GHB. Porrata confirms that the drug is still popular with teens, who use it recreationally. However, it is no longer exclusively a club drug. "Teens don't have to be at a rave," Porrata points out. "It can be used in your own backyard, at frat parties, any party scene."

In addition to locker rooms, house parties, and dance clubs, GHB is also being abused in the modeling industry. Young women intent on staying skinny pass up the calories in alcoholic beverages and instead get high with GHB.

GHB is also being abused in the modeling industry by young women whose livelihood depends upon them staying thin. "It's partying without the calories," explains Porrata.

Finally, some people use GHB as a way to simply forget what they are doing. Strippers working in nightclubs often use GHB as a way to stay thin, to remove their inhibitions about stripping, and to block out thoughts about the way they earn their money.

Porrata continues her mission to educate people about drugs. The news media may report that GHB use is down, and they've moved on to fresher, more sensational stories. And yet, says Porrata, she's busier than ever educating people about the dangers of GHB use.

CHAPTER 3
Coping with GHB Abuse and Seeking Treatment

Patti Trovato Ragano had a son, Matt, who died due to GHB abuse. In an interview with the author, Ragano provided valuable insight into the nature of GHB addiction, the strain it places on the family, and its potentially fatal consequences.

Matt was a small, slender kid looking for a way to be noticed, so he joined the wrestling team at his junior high school. He loved the competition and the rush he got from overpowering his opponents. He especially loved the way his body was beginning to develop. His strength and muscle mass improved, giving him an extra dose of self-confidence. Matt was on his way. His goal was clear. One day, he planned to compete in the Mr. America bodybuilding contest.

Aside from working out with his wrestling teammates, Matt began watching his diet, eating lots of chicken and rice. He became a health fanatic. By the time he turned seventeen, he added weightlifting to his fitness regimen. He became a regular at the local gym. It was here, his mom recalls, that his battle with GHB began.

This was right before the FDA banned GHB, so it was still sold legally in health food stores. The other weightlifters were using Renewtrient, a dietary supplement that included GHB. They encouraged Matt, telling him the supplement was a muscle builder and

Renewtrient and other so-called dietary supplements, such as Renew G *(left)*, have been sold in health food stores and on the Internet. Many of them have been banned from sale by the government. Unfortunately, these illegal drugs are still surfacing underground, promoted as mood enhancers, weight-loss supplements, and anti-aging formulas.

that it was perfectly safe and harmless. Matt would take a capful at night and sleep for hours. The supplement caused him to fall into a period of deep sleep. He believed his muscles were regenerating during this time. Matt considered GHB a fountain of youth drug.

By the time Matt turned twenty, however, his mother believed GHB had totally consumed her son. At this point, GHB use was illegal, but it was still easily available through drug dealers. Her son was now using it daily.

Matt changed. In his mother's eyes, he had been a beautiful boy, but now his physique was almost grotesque. His personality changed, too. When he was using, he became withdrawn and stayed away from the family. He got stopped by the police dozens of times for driving erratically. GHB made him drowsy, and he would doze off at the wheel. The police thought he was driving under the influence, but they never found any alcohol in his blood, so they sent him on his way.

The following year, Matt wound up in the emergency room twelve times due to GHB overdoses. Doctors were puzzled. He appeared to be a healthy, well-nourished bodybuilder. His mother insisted it was the GHB. She'd gone on the Internet and researched the drug herself.

Each time Matt was taken to the hospital, his mother brought the bottle of Renewtrient with her and showed it to the doctors. However, they just shrugged their shoulders. They didn't know much about the supplement at the time, and no traces of drugs were ever found in his body. When Matt woke up, he was cleared to leave the hospital.

Matt spent the next few years trying to quit using GHB, his mom recalled. He'd hand her his paycheck every week, fearing he'd spend it all on GHB. Withdrawal from the drug was unbearable for him, however. "He'd come to me in a cold sweat. The vomiting would start, and he'd tell me he couldn't sleep without the GHB. He'd turned the house upside down looking for it. After another car crash, he ended up in the hospital again. This time the doctor looked at the bottle of Renewtrient and finally listened."

Matt was sent to a treatment facility for three days of detox. Shortly after, his family convinced him to go to a rehabilitation center to defeat his addiction once and for all. Even after thirty days there, however, Matt felt he wasn't ready to come home. "He told me, 'Mom, I can't live like this.' I told him, Matt, I cannot go to your funeral. 'I just want to sleep,' he answered."

At age twenty-six, Matt was found dead in his apartment. His father found him laying flat on his bed. It looked like someone positioned him like that. There were no traces of GHB in the apartment. Nothing was found in his system either. As Patti recalls:

> We wondered if maybe he was trying to quit again, and he just couldn't bear the withdrawal. Maybe he called a friend, looking for something to take the

edge off, something else to help him sleep. When they did the autopsy, they found heroin and cocaine in his body. They call it a speedball. I guess we didn't know the depths of his addiction.

THE ADDICT

According to the National Institute on Drug Abuse (NIDA), drug addiction or dependency is a disease of the brain. The first few times someone experiments with a drug, it may be voluntary. After repeated use, however, some drugs have a way of altering what the NIDA calls the brain's "circuitry." Once someone becomes addicted, the brain changes, and drug abuse is no longer voluntary. It becomes a compulsion.

What's the difference between drug abuse and drug addiction or dependency? Drug abuse is the use of illegal drugs or the misuse of over-the-counter and prescription drugs. Abuse of drugs doesn't necessarily lead to addiction or dependence, though it can result in serious illness and overdose. Addiction or dependency is a repeated and continuing compulsion to use the drug, even if it causes physical and psychological harm to the user and his or her family. The drug is used habitually—often every day or several times a day—and the body gets used to its effects.

Researchers are still unsure of the reasons behind addiction. The composition of the drug itself may bolster addictiveness. A person's genetic makeup may further influence drug dependence.

Anxiety, depression, peer pressure, nutritional deficiencies, and neurotransmitter imbalances may also be contributing factors. A GHB addiction can develop in just a few short weeks. ProjectGHB.org offers this scenario: "From a nightly sleep aid, for example, use casually moves into a morning 'wake up' aid. Then it is needed in the afternoon, to have sex, to go out in public, etc., until it has progressed to around the clock use." Users are still oblivious at this point because they don't see it as a dangerous drug and are still reaping its benefits.

As use of GHB advances, the negative effects start to crop up, including muscle twitching and blackouts. Friends start to notice bizarre behavior. Users start to withdraw from family and friends. Then memory loss occurs. Addicts may wake up one morning and not know where they were the night before or what they've done. One morning, they may simply never wake up. Ingesting too much GHB can slow breathing and nervous system functions to the point that the user falls face down in bed, can't move, and either smothers to death or chokes on his or her own vomit.

WITHDRAWAL AND TREATMENT

Chronic GHB abusers report that withdrawal symptoms can be severe, painful, and terrifying. Withdrawal is characterized by anxiety, psychotic (mentally deranged) thoughts, insomnia (difficulty sleeping), tremors, increased heart rate, and soaring blood pressure. In some cases, addicts going through GHB withdrawal attempt suicide.

A substance abuse treatment advisory prepared by the Department of Health and Human Services (DHHS) states that GHB withdrawal and detoxification require close medical monitoring due to the severity of the process. Hospital stays may range anywhere from seven to fourteen days. Benzodiazepine (an anti–anxiety agent) is thought to help lessen the symptoms of withdrawal when given in medically supervised doses. Other

GHB withdrawal can be harrowing. Soaring blood pressure, suicidal and psychotic thoughts, and anxiety are some of the symptoms described by those in drug rehabilitation. For these reasons, those in treatment must be closely monitored. Counselors work with patients, helping them to set goals for a healthy future.

medications recommended by the DHHS include barbiturates, anticonvulsants, and anti-hypertensives (to manage a racing heart and blood pressure).

Regarding recovery, treatment specialists often rely on "social education modality" as a method of helping a GHB addict get clean. This strategy involves the acquisition of coping skills and better role models, realistic goal setting, skill training, and improved impulse control. Rather than dwell on past mistakes, counselors try to teach recovering addicts practical skills so that they can avoid

GHB Abuse Sweeps the Country

How common and widespread is GHB abuse in the United States? According to data provided by the Drug Abuse Warning Network (DAWN), visits to emergency rooms by GHB users increased from 145 to 3,330 between 1995 and 2002 (with a peak of 4,969 visits in 2000). In the second half of 2003, DAWN estimates that 990 GHB-related emergency room visits occurred. GHB-related deaths occurred in multiple areas of the United States according to a 2002 ONDCP report. In 1999, Texas reported 3 GHB-related deaths, Minnesota reported 2, while Missouri saw 5 deaths and 2 near-deaths in cases in which GHB-fueled date rapes occurred. In 2000, Florida reported 23 deaths in which the presence of GHB was detected. The drug was identified as the definitive cause of death in 6 of those cases. GHB use has been documented in Boston; Detroit; Los Angeles; New York; Seattle; Baltimore; Newark, New Jersey; Washington, D.C.; and nearly every state in the United States. No region of the country is immune from the drug's harmful presence and potentially fatal effects.

future problems. Individuals learn how to live without GHB, move forward, and re-create their lives.

Residential treatment programs that last at least three months seem to have the highest success rates, according to Drug-Rehabs.org, a nonprofit organization that provides information on drug abuse, as well as links to treatment centers for specific addictions. The organization offers this encouragement to try the hard work of rehab: "Three months [of treatment] may seem like a long time, but one day in the life of an individual addicted to GHB can feel like an eternity."

Addiction is an incredibly powerful force to overcome. How is someone weaned off GHB? Doctors are still researching protocols to treat GHB addiction. Yet, a number of treatment professionals believe that the root of addiction—not the specific substance—is the ultimate problem. To help addicts stop their destructive behavior, the root causes of the addiction must be investigated. The stresses and unfulfilled needs that drove the addict to the drug in the first place must be discovered and addressed.

CHAPTER 4
GHB and the Legal System

GHB has been outlawed since February 18, 2000, when former President Bill Clinton signed the "Hillory J. Farias and Samantha Reid Date-Rape Prevention Act" into law.

As briefly discussed in chapter 1, following the enactment of the new law, GHB became a Schedule I Controlled Substance. The ONDCP defines drugs in this category as having "a high potential for abuse" and no recognized medical value. They are also considered to be unsafe even under medical supervision.

There is one exception in which GHB can be used legally, for a legitimate medical purpose. In 2002, the FDA approved the medical use of Xyrem—a prescription drug containing sodium oxybate or GHB—for patients afflicted with narcolepsy, a disorder

Dr. Martin Scharf *(above)*, of the Tri-State Sleep Disorders Center in Cincinnati, Ohio, has prescribed GHB for his patients who suffer from narcolepsy. In 2002, Xyrem, a prescription drug containing GHB, was approved by the U.S. Food and Drug Administration for use in treating this disorder.

that brings on sudden, uncontrolled periods of sleep. Xyrem is categorized as a Schedule III Controlled Substance, meaning it has less potential for abuse than Schedule I drugs, including GHB on its own. It is the only drug containing GHB that is legally approved for use in the United States. In a report, the FDA declared that Xyrem would be made available by prescription only, through a "restricted distribution program." Misuse or illegal sales of the prescription drug can result in criminal penalties.

ARRESTS AND CONSEQUENCES

Those who use GHB for illegal (or legal) purposes are subject to Schedule I penalties. In other words, if you possess, manufacture, or distribute GHB, you can face up to twenty years in prison. Various criminal charges may be imposed, depending on the circumstances of the case. Penalties vary from state to state. A person could be charged with possession, possession for sale, poisoning, and even manslaughter or homicide if the sale and use of the drug results in a fatality. Penalties are severe for those who use GHB in sexual assaults. However, according to the DEA, these crimes are hard to prosecute for the following reasons:

- The victim may be completely unaware that his or her drink was spiked with GHB, since it is a clear, odorless liquid.
- GHB use impairs memory. The victim may not even be aware of the sexual assault until eight to twelve hours after it happened or be able to recall who abused him or her.
- GHB is metabolized quickly. Routine blood and urine tests do not screen for GHB. A victim who suspects that his or her drink was spiked and that he or she was sexually attacked should request a GHB screening test. Otherwise, there may be very little physical evidence to support the claim that a crime has been committed.

Those who use GHB for illegal purposes face stiff penalties such as twenty years in prison. Andrew Luster *(left)*, heir to the Max Factor cosmetics fortune, is seen here following his 2003 arrest for drugging and raping three women.

The U.S. government has had some success monitoring and cracking down on the illegal use of GHB. Between March 1999 and January 2000, two brothers, running an Internet business selling GHB kits, were tracked by the New Jersey Statewide Narcotics Task Force. The kits were being sold as computer-cleaning solvents. Undercover agents purchased the kits, which were found to include instructions and ingredients to make GHB from GBL. Each kit, selling for $55, contained enough ingredients to make as much as twenty doses. During the police raid, a 55-gallon drum of GBL plus ten pounds (4.5 kilograms) of sodium hydroxide were seized. The men were sentenced to four years in a New Jersey prison, under a plea agreement.

On September 19, 2002, more than 100 people in eighty-four cities across the United States and Canada were arrested for distributing GHB and its analogs, GBL and BD, via the Internet. The arrests were the result of Operation Webslinger, a two-year multi-agency investigation conducted by the DEA and others, including the U.S. Postal Inspection Service, Internal Revenue Service (IRS), Federal Bureau of Investigation (FBI), and the Royal Canadian Mounted Police (RCMP). The U.S. Department of Justice reports that of the 115 people arrested, 27 were wholesale distributors. Others included a physician, a former teacher, and a former police officer.

Drug Abuse and the Domino Effect

Juveniles (kids under age eighteen) accounted for more than 1.9 million arrests for drug violations between 1994 and 2003, according to data provided by the U.S. Department of Justice's Uniform Crime Reporting Program. The arrests were mainly for possession, rather than sale or manufacture of drugs.

When teens and adults use drugs for their own pleasure, to satisfy their curiosity, or for excitement, the consequences may be far-reaching and destructive, negatively affecting the lives of innocent people. Those who abuse drugs and drive under the influence kill innocent people on the road every day. Children whose mothers and fathers deal and/or use drugs are robbed of a stable home life when their parents are convicted and sent to jail. The government and taxpayers are saddled with the growing costs of drug treatment programs, health care, and incarceration (jailing) of convicted drug offenders. A drug abuser's problem becomes everyone's problem.

In 2002, Attorney General John Ashcroft announces a nation-wide drug crackdown known as "Operation Webslinger." Internet traffickers in eighty-four cities in the U.S. and Canada were arrested for distributing GHB and its analogs, GBL and BD. The two-year criminal investigation was conducted by various governmental agencies and rounded up 115 people, including 27 wholesale distributors.

REFORM: JAIL OR DRUG COURT?

GHB addicts and other drug abusers who are facing jail terms but are serious about getting clean may benefit from a drug court program. The first such courts were established during the 1980s. According to the U.S. Department of Justice, there are hundreds of drug courts across the United States today. Participants undergo long-term treatment, counseling, and ongoing court appearances. If a user successfully completes the program, he or she earns a fresh start, with dismissal of charges, lesser penalties, or reduced sentences. Participants also walk away, prepared to start a new, drug-free life.

CHAPTER 5

The Impact of Drug Abuse on Society

Drug abuse can become so over-whelming that friends, family, academics, sports, and even your health no longer matter to you. Drug abuse is a serious problem, one you probably cannot fix on your own, even though you may want to believe you can.

If you steal in order to finance your drug habit and get arrested, it becomes a problem for the legal system. If you crash the family car while driving under the influence, it becomes a problem for your parents. That problem trickles down to their insurance carrier, who will raise your parents' auto rates. If you cut school, neglect assignments, and bring home failing grades due to drug use, you run the risk of jeopardizing your acceptance into the college of your choice or not being able to attend

Drugs can impair your judgment and negatively affect your senses and reaction time. Statistics show that substance abusers are responsible for 50 percent of deaths on U.S. highways. If you choose to drive while under the influence and get into an accident, you may not harm only yourself. Friends, family, and innocent strangers may die because of your poor choices.

college at all. This, in turn, could mean that future employment and earning opportunities may be limited.

Therefore, drug abuse in America, in one way or another, impacts everyone.

The economic cost of drug abuse to U.S. society has been estimated to be in the billions of dollars. According to the National Institute on Drug Abuse, the costs keep increasing for several reasons. Cocaine and crack cocaine are more readily available. HIV infection among intravenous drug users (those who use needles to inject drugs into their bloodstream) continues to spread. The number of people treated for alcohol abuse who also have drug abuse problems continues to increase. Support and treatment for substance abuse has become more available, and health-care services for drug abuse have become more accessible. Although this last development is a positive one, it's also an expensive one, with a bill that is mainly footed by taxpayers.

THE IMPACT ON THE FAMILY

Drug abuse can turn family life upside down. Parents and siblings will notice a sharp change in the user's personality. Mood swings become commonplace. The user may seem depressed, withdrawing from family activities. Lies become the norm. A user may pretend to still hang out with school friends, when he or she has since dumped them for drug buddies. Schoolwork usually suffers, grades fall, interest in extra-curricular activities, like sports or music, wanes. Physically, the user's grooming and hygiene may start to suffer. The addict may begin to look disheveled and may drop some weight. Eventually, parents begin to focus only on their drug-abusing child, and the rest of the family gets neglected. The house fills with anger, resentment, and fear.

DRUGS AND PRISON

Here are some facts to consider concerning drug offenses and imprisonment:

- 2002—The total number of inmates in federal, state, and county prisons across the United States totaled 440,670. Of those, 112,447 were drug offenders: 48,823 inmates were convicted of possession, while 56,574 were found guilty of trafficking.
- 2003—The number of convicted drug offenders in federal prisons grew to 86,972, up from 52,782 in 1995.
- 2003—According to the budget summary of the Office of National Drug Control Policy, the cost to the federal government to incarcerate drug offenders is approaching $3 billion a year.

DRUGS AND COMMUNITY

Drug abuse doesn't only affect the user and his or her family. It can also have direct and indirect consequences—often fatal—for many innocent victims.

Statistics show that substance abusers account for 50 percent of deaths on U.S. highways. Substance abuse causes occupational accidents. Injured employees lose time on the job. Employers, in turn, must replace and train new employees. Drug abusers who

Innocent people suffer when drug abuse surfaces in their communities. Drugs breed crime, home invasions, gun violence, and muggings. Decent, hardworking people trying to raise families suffer when their neighborhood's reputation is tainted by drug abuse. This drug-infested street in West Philadelphia is now home to boarded-up houses and drug dens. Most residents who had somewhere else to go have fled.

lose their jobs may force their families to turn to welfare, putting a financial strain on the government. Drug abuse breeds crime. Home invasions, muggings, and gun violence increase, giving good neighborhoods bad reputations. As a result, real estate values drop and the streetscape degenerates, leading to a downward spiral of further poverty, violence, and drug abuse.

DRUG ADDICTION AND PARENTING: A LETHAL COMBINATION

The National Clearinghouse on Child Abuse and Neglect studied substance abuse and its impact on the child welfare system. In 2003, it was estimated that approximately six million children live with a parent who abuses alcohol or drugs. The study found that these kids are more likely to suffer from physical, sexual, and emotional abuse than children who live in homes where there are no substance-abusing parents. Children of substance abusers may miss out on the basics of proper nutrition, adult supervision, and simple nurturing.

Sadly, children of substance-abusing parents are at high risk of eventually developing substance-abuse problems themselves. They are more likely to grow up to victimize their own children due to their drug abuse.

CHAPTER 6
GHB and the Media

It's hard not to get tangled up and confused by the web of information we're bombarded with each and every day. You'd have to live under a rock not to be influenced in some way by the media. With the glut of round-the-clock news, entertainment, and commercial messages people receive via television, radio, the Internet, newspapers, and magazines, it's no wonder kids and adults feel overwhelmed when making decisions that affect their well-being.

On one hand, advertisers promote over-the-counter and prescription drugs that promise a good night's sleep or something to help you relax in social situations. There are prescription drugs that boost concentration, lift depression, and help you lose weight. There seems to be a cure for whatever ails America, and some kids find these promises of a quick fix very alluring. Many teenagers try to emulate their favorite rail-thin celebrities by starving themselves or taking diet supplements. Young athletes watch professional athletes break records and wonder if maybe steroids aren't so bad after all.

Freevibe.com, a Web site that provides teens with facts on drugs, describes how some kids feel about the media's messages. "Seeing pictures of rich and beautiful people all the time gives

Sometimes, the media makes the drug culture look hip and romantic. Drug lords, like Al Pacino's character in the 1983 movie *Scarface (above)*, are often portrayed as slick, well-dressed, and living the good life. Some kids may get the impression that drugs may put them on the road to fame and fortune. It's important to have a clear-eyed understanding of the likely consequences of involvement in the drug trade as either a seller, buyer, or user.

them feelings of low self-esteem. They feel they can't really be happy unless they're like those people: thin, or rich, or constantly partying, or whatever. They believe the hype, and do anything—including drugs—to get there." Freevibe offers the following questions to help you sort out for yourself what's real and what's just hype in the drug messages you're receiving from the media:

- When you watch television commercials or read magazine advertisements, think about what is being sold. Are the manufacturers and advertisers promoting a product or an entire lifestyle? Do they seem to be promising that you'll be a better person if you use it?
- When you listen to music, think about the lyrics. Write them down and read them out loud without the music playing in the background. What are they really saying? What sort of behavior is being encouraged, romanticized, or glorified? Is this behavior that is likely to lead to your long-term happiness or physical, mental, and emotional health?
- When you go online, read the posted information carefully and critically. Consider who may have created the site, what their agenda may be, and whether the information they are passing along is factual and accurate.

GHB IN THE NEWS

The media isn't always promoting irresponsible messages about drug use. In fact, the media can be a valuable and informative

Top Ten Facts About GHB

1. GHB (gamma hydroxybutyrate) is a clear, odorless, slightly salty liquid drug that acts as a central nervous system depressant. It has a sedative effect, making the user feel sleepy.

2. GHB has been outlawed since 2000. It is a Schedule I Controlled Substance. If you possess, manufacture, or distribute GHB, you can face up to twenty years in prison.

3. GHB is a dangerous drug. Its analogs, GBL (gamma butyrolactone) and BD (1,4 butanediol), are equally dangerous. Even if taken in small doses, these drugs can be lethal, depending on their purity and strength.

4. GHB use can provoke the following reported side effects: nausea, vomiting, vertigo (dizziness), hallucinations, seizures, amnesia, loss of consciousness, and coma.

5. GHB is addictive. When used daily, an addiction can occur within two months. Researchers have found that withdrawal symptoms can begin between one and six hours after the last dose.

6. GHB mixed with alcohol can be fatal.

7. Because GHB can cause drowsiness and unconsciousness in unknowing victims, sexual predators have been known to use GHB as a date-rape drug, especially in bars, clubs, and house and campus parties.

8. Some street names for GHB include Liquid X, G, Georgia Home Boy, Scoop, and Cherry Meth.

9. Some street names for the GHB analogs GBL and BD include Blue Nitro, Revivarant, and Enliven.

10. Scientists are still studying the long-term effects of GHB abuse, but they believe it may be capable of altering memory and learning functions.

source in the struggle against drug abuse. A 2003 study by the Ohio Department of Alcohol and Drug Addiction Services suggested that because of the media's efforts to publicize the dangers of GHB, use was down in that state. Club drug users interviewed said the media's messages about negative experiences with the drug, coupled with peer-to-peer warnings about its dangers, had led to a decline in use.

People rely on news organizations to keep informed about global issues, health advances, and government studies. In the case of GHB, word got out that this is a very dangerous drug. You can find ongoing news reports of arrests, date rapes, overdoses, and GHB-related deaths in newspapers across the United States.

In 2000 and 2001, the *New York Daily News* ran a

Read labels critically and don't be fooled by false claims that make promises that are too good to be true. Remember that your health is more important than a short-lived high or the quest for a "ripped" body. Rely on newspapers, television, and reputable medical Internet sources that offer objective, intelligent reporting on issues that affect your physical and emotional growth.

series of articles warning sports and fitness buffs about the documented dangers of GHB. Recovering GHB addicts were interviewed about the severity of withdrawal symptoms and the long, tough road to recovery. Toxicologists commented on the possibility of a GHB epidemic. Parents of GHB users who died due to the use of the drug were interviewed about its addictive qualities and harmful side effects. Even athletic trainers confirmed the prevalence of GHB abuse in professional sports circles. These articles did more than simply spew facts and figures. They showed how GHB abuse affects real lives.

Drug consultant Trinka Porrata is an expert on GHB abuse. Porrata has appeared on such network television programs as *Good Morning America* and *20/20*, speaking out about the drug. She has been consulted for articles that have appeared in *Newsweek* and *U.S. News and World Report*, as well as *Glamour*, *Family Circle*, and *Seventeen* magazines. She believes the media must continue reporting the dangers of GHB. People need to realize that this drug is more pervasive than they know, she explains, and therefore the danger is greater than they believe. "This is just the tip of the iceberg," she warns.

BEING INFORMED, GETTING HELP, AND STAYING SAFE

GHB abuse remains a significant problem. However, now you know the facts. You are now aware of the health risks, legal consequences, and emotional scarring associated with GHB abuse, both for the user and his or her innocent victims, including friends and family members. When it comes to drugs, get the facts, think for yourself, and always be safe. In closing, here are some tips to keep in mind:

- Never leave your drink unattended. Ask a trusted friend to watch your drink if you need to leave the area momentarily.
- Don't take a drink from a punchbowl. It might be spiked.
- Don't accept a drink from someone you don't know or trust, whether it's alcoholic or not.
- If you wake up and feel like you may have been drugged and/or sexually assaulted, go to the hospital as soon as possible, without showering or bathing first. GHB leaves the body quickly, but if you hurry, it may still be detectable in your urine. Showering or bathing may wash away crucial evidence of a sexual assault.
- If someone you know passes out after ingesting GHB, turn the person on his or her side to keep from choking on his or her vomit. Help save your friend's life by calling 911 immediately. Be direct and frank when telling the 911 operator and medical personnel about what has been ingested, when, and how much.
- If you suspect that you have a drug problem, talk to someone you trust and get help.

GLOSSARY

analog A derivative of a parent compound that usually differs from it by one element.

BD (1,4 butanediol) An analog that is converted by the body into GHB.

central nervous system The portion of the human body that consists of the brain and spinal chord.

club drugs A variety of drugs often used at all-night dances, concerts, and nightclubs.

coma A state of unconsciousness caused by poison, disease, or injury.

date rape A forcible sexual act committed by someone known to the victim. Also known as acquaintance rape.

detoxification (detox) In the case of a drug user, to free the body of an addictive substance or from addiction to such a substance.

dietary supplement A product, other than food, that is intended to supplement one's diet. It is taken orally (through the mouth).

dosage The application of a drug or medicine in a measured quantity.

drug addiction A disease of the brain that causes an ongoing compulsion to use drugs, despite physical and psychological harm to the user.

euphoria A feeling of well-being or elation.

GBL (gamma butyrolactone) An analog that is converted by the body into GHB. It is an industrial solvent.

GHB (gamma-hydroxybutyrate) An illegal drug characterized by its colorless, odorless, slightly salty taste.

overdose The taking of an excessive amount of a drug or medicine, which can be toxic or even lethal.

Schedule I Controlled Substance Schedule I categorization is reserved for the most dangerous drugs that have no recognized medical use. GHB falls into this category.

withdrawal The physical and psychological symptoms that follow discontinuance of an addictive substance.

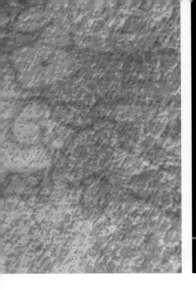

FOR MORE INFORMATION

Centers for Disease Control
  and Prevention
1600 Clifton Road
Atlanta, GA 30333
(800) CDC-INFO (232-4636)
Web site: http://www.cdc.gov

Drug Policy Information
  Clearinghouse
P.O. Box 6000
Rockville, MD 20849–6000
(800) 666–3332
Web site: http://www.
  whitehousedrugpolicy.org

Narcotics Anonymous
World Service Office in
  Los Angeles

P.O. Box 9999
Van Nuys, CA 91409
(818) 773-9999
Web site: http://www.na.org

Partnership for a Drug-Free
  America
405 Lexington Avenue,
  Suite 1601
New York, NY 10174
(212) 922-1560
Web site: http://www.
  drugfree.org

The Rape, Abuse & Incest
  National Network (RAINN)
2000 L Street NW, Suite 406
Washington, DC 20036

(800) 656-HOPE (4673)
Web site: http://www.
  rainn.org

StreetDrugs.org
Publishers Group, LLC
2805 Alvarado Lane North
Plymouth, MN 55447
(763) 473-0646
Web site: http://www.
  streetdrugs.org

Substance Abuse and Mental
Health Services Administration
1 Choke Cherry Road,
  Room 8-1036
Rockville, MD 20857
(800) 273-8255
Web site: http://www.
  samhsa.gov

U.S. Drug Enforcement
  Administration
2401 Jefferson Davis Highway
Alexandria, VA 22301
(800) 882-9539
Web site: http://www.dea.gov

WEB SITES

Due to the changing nature
of Internet links, the Rosen
Publishing Group, Inc., has
developed an online list of
Web sites related to the subject of this book. This site is
updated regularly. Please use
this link to access the list:

http://www.rosenlinks.com/
  das/ghba

FOR FURTHER READING

Balkin, Karen F., ed. *Club Drugs.* Farmington Hills, MI: Greenhaven, 2005.

Barrett, Cece. *The Dangers of Diet Drugs and Other Weight-Loss Products.* New York, NY: Rosen Publishing Group, 1999.

Bellenir, Karen, ed. *Drug Information for Teens: Health Tips About the Physical and Mental Effects of Substance Abuse.* Detroit, MI: Omnigraphics, 2002.

Clayton, Lawrence. *Designer Drugs.* New York, NY: Rosen Publishing Group, 1998.

Columbia University's Health Education Program. *The "Go Ask Alice" Book of Answers: A Guide to Good Physical, Sexual, and Emotional Health.* New York, NY: Henry Holt, 1998.

Fooks, Louie. *The Drug Trade: The Impact on Our Lives.* Chicago, IL: Raintree, 2003.

Moe, Barbara A. *Drug Abuse Relapse: Helping Teens to Get Clean Again.* New York, NY: Rosen Publishing Group, 2000.

Monroe, Judy. *Steroids, Sports, and Body Image: The Risks of Performance-Enhancing Drugs.* Berkeley Heights, NJ: Enslow Publishers, 2004.

Packer, Alex J. *Highs!: Over 150 Ways to Feel Really, Really Good . . . Without Alcohol or Other Drugs.* Minneapolis, MN: Free Spirit Publishing, 2000.

Parker, James N., and Philip M. Parker, eds. *The Official Patient's Sourcebook on GHB Dependence: A Revised and Updated Directory for the Internet Age.* San Diego, CA: Icon Health Publications, 2002.

Patrick, Regina. "GHB and Narcolepsy." *FOCUS: Journal for Respiratory Care & Sleep Medicine*, Summer 2003.

Rinaldo, Denise. "The Party's Over." *Scholastic Choices*, January 1, 2004.

BIBLIOGRAPHY

"Club Drugs." Drug Facts: Office of National Drug Control Policy. January 2006. Retrieved March 2006 (http://www.whitehousedrugpolicy.gov/drugfact/club/index.html).

"Drug Abuse and Dependence." MedlinePlus. October 2005. Retrieved March 2006 (http://www.nlm.nih.gov/medlineplus/ency/article/001522.htm).

"Drugs and Chemicals of Concern: Gamma Hydroxybutyric Acid." Office of Diversion Control. July 2004. Retrieved March 2006 (http://www.deadiversion.usdoj.gov/drugs_concern/ghb/ghb.htm).

"Gamma Hydroxybutyrate (GHB)." Office of National Drug Control Policy: Drug Policy Information Clearinghouse. November 2002. Retrieved March 2006 (http://www.whitehousedrugpolicy.gov/publications/factsht/gamma).

"Gamma Hydroxy Butyrate Use—New York and Texas, 1995-1996." *Morbidity and Mortality Weekly Report*, April 1997, pp. 281-283.

National Clearinghouse for Alcohol and Drug Information. "GHB: A Club Drug to Watch." *Substance Abuse Treatment Advisory: Breaking News for the Treatment Field.* Vol. 2, No. 1 (November 2002): 1–4.

"GHB." Brown University Health Education. 2004. Retrieved January 2006 (http://www.brown.edu/Student_Services/ Health_Services/Health_Education/atod/od_ghb.htm).

"GHB." DrugAbuseHelp.com. Retrieved March 2006 (http:// www.drugabusehelp.com/drugs/ghb).

"GHB Myths Exposed: Have You Been Looking for Some Truth About GHB?" Project GHB. Retrieved March 2006 (http://www.projectGHB.org/ghbtruth.htm).

Goldstein, Avram. *Addiction: From Biology to Drug Policy.* New York, NY: Oxford University Press, 2001.

Landry, Mim J. *Understanding Drugs of Abuse: The Processes of Addiction, Treatment, and Recovery.* Washington, DC: American Psychiatric Publishing, 1994.

"Medical Consequences of Drug Abuse." National Institute on Drug Abuse. June 2005. Retrieved March 2006 (http:// www.nida.nih.gov/consequences).

Miller, Norman S., ed. *Comprehensive Handbook of Drug and Alcohol Addiction.* New York, NY: Dekker, 1991.

O'Connell, Ted, Lily Kaye, and John J. Plosay III. "Gamma-Hydroxybutyrate (GHB): A Newer Drug of Abuse." *American Family Physician.* December 1, 2000. Retrieved March 2006 (http://www.aafp.org/afp/20001201/2478.html).

Perkins, Scott W. *Drug Identification: Designer and Club Drugs Quick Reference Guide.* Carrolton, TX: Alliance Press, 2000.

Porrata, Trinka. "GHB Addiction & Withdrawal Syndrome Fact Sheet." Project GHB. Retrieved March 2006 (http://www.projectGHB.org/files/addictionfactsheet.htm).

Porrata, Trinka, telephone interview with the author, December 2005.

Ragano, Patti Trovto, telephone interview with the author, December 2005.

Salamone, Salvatore J., ed. *Benzodiazepines and GHB: Detection and Pharmacology.* Totowa, NJ: Humana Press, 2001.

SAMHSA, Office of Applied Studies. "Drug Abuse Warning Network (DAWN), 2003: Interim National Estimates of Drug-Related Emergency Department Visits." Rockville, MD: U.S. Department of Health and Human Serives, 2004.

"Substance Abuse." Recovery Connection. Retrieved March 2006 (http://www.recoveryconnection.org/substance_abuse).

Swan, Neil. "Drug Abuse Cost to Society Set at $97.7 Billion, Continuing Steady Increase Since 1975." *NIDA Notes* November 1998.

"What Is GHB?" Project GHB. Retrieved March 2006 (http://www.projectGHB.org/english.htm).

"Why People Take Drugs." Freevibe.com. Retrieved March 2006 (http://www.freevibe.com/Drug_Facts/why_drugs.asp).

INDEX

ABOUT THE AUTHOR

Marie E. Wolf is a New York–based writer, former parenting magazine editor, and the mother of three children. For the past twenty years, she has written newspaper and magazine articles focusing on family matters, health, and fitness, covering such topics as child molestation, juvenile fire-starters, and cyber bullies. As a parent and as a writer who has spoken to many parents and teens, Wolf has found there is no greater heartbreak than that of a parent who has lost a child to drugs. The author hopes that through this book, students, educators, and parents will gather and share vital information about the dangers of the drug GHB, thereby preventing further tragedies.

PHOTO CREDITS

Pp. 5, 11, 12, 35, 39, 44 © AP/Wide World Photos; p. 9 © AFP/Getty Images; p. 17 © Stephen Hird/Reuters/Corbis; p. 22 © Scott Halleran/Getty Images; p. 23 © Ted Soqui/Corbis; p. 31 © Tom Stewart/Corbis; p. 37 © Getty Images; p. 41 © www.istockphoto.com/Frances Twitty; p. 47 © Universal/courtesy Everett Collection; p. 50 © Najlah Feanny/Corbis Saba.

Designer: Tahara Anderson: Photo Researcher: Nicole DiMella